Based on Board/University Syllabus for all other

Computer/Competitive Exams

Learn

WINDOWS

Dr. Suhas S. Rokde

MCM, Ph.D.(Astro.Sci.)

Director : Astro-Tech Research Lab

Publication : Paperback Publication

Edition : 2014, 2015, 2018

Website : www.astrotechlab.com

Email : info@astrotechlab.com

A gift for my students

Index...

WINDOWS Operating System

- Introduction
- Advantage of Windows
- Advantages of Windows
- Advantages of Windows
- Basic Windows Accessories
- Notepad
- MS-Paint
- Calculator
- WordPad
- Creating Shortcuts
- Windows Explorer

Learn Windows

📁 Control Panel

📁 Add New Hardware

📁 Add Or Remove Programs

📁 Date and Time

📁 My Computer

📁 My Documents

📁 Recycle Bin

📁 Screen Saver

📁 Wallpaper

📁 System Tools

📁 Backup

📁 Disk Cleanup

📁 Disk Defragmenter

📁 Files and Settings Transfer Wizard

📁 Scheduled Tasks overview

📁 Character Map

Learn Windows

📂 System Information

📂 System Restore Overview

📂 Security Center

📂 Firewall

📂 Virus Protection

📂 Automatic Updates

📂 Setting peripherals

📂 Setting up a Printer

📂 New features in Windows version

📂 Installing Software

📂 Features of Windows

📂 Features of Vista versions

📂 IMP Questions

Author's overview...

As an author is a man of few words. He finished his PG in Computer Management and Doctorate in Astrology. He has written more than 24 books, which published by well-known  publisher along with Top International online publisher as Amazon, Google. He has born in cultured & educated family. He is a first class student from childhood. He lost his father at the age of sixteenth. He wisely handled all responsibility of his family & started further education as 'Learning & Earning' mode. He played a vital role in well-known IT organization. He is now consulting his worldwide clients in Technology & Spiritual Science.

His book appreciated by worldwide reader. His success secret key is "Nothing is impossible to a willing mind".

Author

Thanks...

My Dear Students,

I am very much thankful to all my readers who like this book. I am take utmost care to include all syllabus contents in this one. It's not easy task.

Actually, a book is not a single person activity. There are many blessing of some elders as my mother & my late father too. I can finish this work under divine power of my Sadgurudeo Nikhileshwaranandaji.

I heartily thanks to all my beloved who directly & indirectly help me to finish a book.

Author

WINDOWS
OPERATING SYSTEM

INTRODUCTION

Window is a GUI (Graphical User Interface) based operating system developed by the Microsoft Corporation. This developed on based on graphics concept. Due to this, feature this operating system more popular among the computer user. This operating system provide joyful environment during the operating. It is more interactive with the user during the operating. All other application easily install with this system and due to this is very helpful to invent new idea of work. Window95, 98, 2000, XP, Media Center, Vista, Win-7, Win-8 & latest version is Windows 10 are a series of up-gradation of the operating system. Some important **features of Windows** operating system is as under.

1) Multi-tasking

2) Multi-user

3) Hardware Support

4) Reliable

5) GUI

Introduction to Windows

The windows and windows for workgroups operating systems provided a graphical environment, networking and performance enhancements to the MS-DOS operating system.

Learn Windows

Microsoft Windows is a truly easy graphical interface that makes it simpler to use your PC while at the same time more efficient and customizable.

The Windows operating system can run your current MS-DOS based and Windows-based programs in a more stable environment.

Windows also offers enhanced multimedia, powerful mobile features and integrated networking.

ADVANTAGE OF WINDOWS

1. Easiest Windows Operating System Yet

❖ Navigate your system quickly with powerful new tools:

❖ Plug and play frees you from manually setting up hardware devices. Windows detects and configures plug and play compatible devices automatically.

❖ Customize and use resources efficiently just click the right mouse button wherever you are working and a context menu appears in order to help you manipulate objects directly.

2. A faster, more powerful Windows

❖ Increase your productivity. A 32-bit architecture delivers better performance and reliability in areas such as networking, printing communicating and multimedia.

❖ Work on several tasks at once. With fast, new 32-bit programs that support multitasking, multithreading, and run in their own memory space, so other programs cannot affect one another.

❖ Focus on your documents instead of the programs that created them. Programs use OLE. Microsoft allows you to create and edit documents easily, allowing you to work not only within a single document, but also within multiple programs.

❖ Built-in networking, Windows is network-ready, providing easy 32-bit, 64-bit access to network resources, even simultaneously.

3. Compatibility in built-in

It works with all your current software, increase control of the desktop. It has centralized security, remote administration and a registry that stores each user's environment. Windows reduces the complexity of remote computing with built-in dial-up networking and support for Plug and Play hardware.

4. **Multiprocessing** – In this case, applications run at the same time, independently of each other.

5. **Flexibility** – no DOS required, and can run on a wider variety of machines

6. **Internet access capabilities is built in**

7. **Easy hardware upgrades using the new standard Plug and Play.**

ADVANTAGES OF WINDOWS

Windows is a hybrid 16/32-bit operating system. It has quite low system requirements; therefore, it can gain full potential even on older machines.

If installed on a bare hard drive, Window 98 uses the FAT32 file system. If supports FAT16 and FAT12 for compatibility with floppy disks. It created with older versions of Windows and with MS-DOS. I/O is on disks larger than 128 GB. It originally not supported, but there are external solutions to this. FAT32 does not support file encryption or file sizes bigger than 2 GB, unlike NTFS, a file system, that, at the time of Windows's release, was only available in professional versions of Windows.

The graphical user interface (GUI) runs on a DOS-based layer. This is partially an advantage and disadvantage. DOS has some limits (such as the number of disk buffers or simultaneously opened files), but through its environment memory managers, drivers or other applications can be loaded which can improve overall system performance and functionality.

Windows also offers full support for DOS applications in the form of being able to boot in "DOS Mode" (MS-DOS can be booted without booting Windows or putting the CPU in protected mode). This differs from the emulation used in Windows NT-based operating systems in that the latter cannot handle devices such as modern or LAN Cards, which are required for some DOS applications.

Since DOS programs provide their own device drivers, some DOS programs, such as those that require a Sound Blaster compatible sound card, cannot run on newer computers without Windows (Which provides Sound Blaster emulation in some sound card drivers).

LAN cards that are not NE2000 compatible generally cannot use at all by DOS programs, with or without Windows.

DOS Mode also offers the ability to fix certain system errors without entering the GUI. E.g. if a virus is active in GUI mode it can often be safely removed in DOS mode, by deleting its executable files, which usually cannot run without Windows. While in "DOS Mode", the 32-bit Windows layer can started with the same DOS command that was used for older versions of Windows going back to Windows 1.0:WIN.COM

The biggest advantage of this operating system is its compatibility with older versions of Windows and MS-DOS. It can successfully run very old applications that have written for Windows 3.0, while also being able to run new applications and applications written for Windows NT.

Another advantage is its small size in comparison to newer Microsoft operating systems. New version required large disk space. Windows can be installing requiring less than 250 MB of HDD space, offering more room for applications and files. It also has a very small memory footprint, so it does not reduce the overall system performance the way current OS do on older systems. When installed on newer systems, Windows SE can boot within 15 seconds and shut down within 3 seconds, giving it a huge advantage in speed when comparing it to current versions of Windows.

ADVANTAGES OF WINDOWS

Both users and developers have been anxiously awaiting the release of Windows. Windows represents a number of milestones in the evolution of the Windows operating system. This is the first version of a Win32 based operating system that intended for both home and business use. Windows includes a number of improvements of the base operating system as well as a number of new accessories that improve the user experience. The most obvious change in Windows is the new shell with its radical new look, revised Start menu, and updated task bar, the new look is based on the ability of Windows to be "skinned." Allowing the user interface to be radically changed with distributable theme files.

Another new feature of Windows is fast user switching that allows multiple users logged onto their own sessions at the same time on the same machine. Clear Type, the Microsoft font display technology for LCD screens, and the successor to Graphical Device Interface (GDI), called GDI+, are also new. The control panel even has a new categorization scheme to make it easy for users to find the control panel applet they need.

These new features will be a boon to users, but they will also influence how you design your apps. Windows goes to great lengths to be compatible with legacy apps, but there are new features that might require workarounds. In addition, there are some new features you should take advantage of when designing your app.

Using different windows applications simultaneously

Click the taskbar button for the program you want to open.

E.g., suppose you want to work with two applications say paint and notepad follows the following steps:

Click on start - > programs - > accessories - > paint

Click on start - > programs - > accessories - > notepad

After following above steps, though you opened two applications, you can work on any one application at a time. The application, which is active currently, will be notepad. To switch to paint, click the paint application to make it active.

Graphical user interface (GUI)

Program interface takes advantage of the computer's graphics capabilities to make the program easier to use. Well-designed graphical user interfaces can free the user from learning complex command languages. On the other hand, many users find that they work more effectively with a command-driven interface, especially if they already know the command language.

Learn Windows

Graphical user interfaces, such as Microsoft Windows and the one used by the Apple Macintosh, feature the following basic components :

1.   Pointer : A symbol that appears on the display screen and that you move to select objects and commands. Usually, the pointer appears as a small angled arrow. Text –processing applications, however, use an I-beam pointer that shaped like a capital I.

2. Pointing device : A device, such as a mouse or trackball, that enables you to select objects on the display screen.

3. Icons : Small pictures that represent commands, files, or windows. By moving the pointer to the icon and pressing a mouse button, you can execute a command or convert the icon into a window. You can also move the icons around the display screen as if they were real objects on your desk.

4. Desktop : The area on the display screen where icons are grouped is often referred to as the desktop because the icons are intended to represent real objects on a real desktop.

5. Windows : You can divide the screen into different areas. In each window, you can run a different program or display a different file. You can move windows around the display screen, and change their shape and size at will.

6. Menus : Most graphical user interfaces let you execute commands by selecting a choice from a menu. The first graphical user interface was designed by Xerox corporation's Palo Alto Research Center in the 1970s, but it was not until the 1980s and the emergence of the Apple Macintosh that graphical user interfaces became popular. One reason for their slow acceptance was the fact that they require considerable CPU power and a high quality monitor, which until recently were prohibitively expensive.

In addition to their visual components, graphical user interfaces also make it easier to move data from one application to another. A true GUI includes standard formats for representing text and graphics. Because the formats are well-define different programs that run under a common GUI can share data. This makes it possible, for example, to copy a graph created by a spreadsheet program into a document created by a word processor.

Many DOS programs include some features of GUIs, such as menus, but are not graphics based. Such interfaces called graphical character-based user interfaces to distinguish them from true GUIs.

Getting Help

Online Help is essential to learning and using windows. There are two kinds of Help. Help about a specific procedure and help that gives you information about what you see on your screen.

To get help :

Click the start button and then click help option.

The list of help topics appears. You can use the tabs in Help to search for information in

Learn Windows

Important Point

When you open Help by using the start menu, or the help menu in my computer or Windows Explorer, you see Help for windows in general. If you use the Help menu in a program, such as WordPad, Paint or Microsoft Word, the help you see is for that program.

To find help through the contents, do the following :

1. Click the contents to find topics grouped by subject and then follow the instructions on your screen.
2. To return to the list of topics click help Topics.
3. To find Help through the Index, do the following : Click the index tab to find specific topics listed alphabetically and then follow the instructions on your screen.

4. To return to the list of topics, click Help Topics.

5. To get help on a specific item, do the following :

6. For information about an item in a dialog box, click question mark (?) and then click the item.

7. A pop-up explanation appears. Click it to make it disappears.

8.

BASIC WINDOWS ACCESSORIES

NOTEPAD

Notepad is one of the most common text-only editors. The resulting files – typically saved with the .txt extension – have no format tags or styles, making the program suitable for editing system files that used in a DOS environment. Notepad can edit files of almost any format; however, it does not treat Unix-style text files correctly,

Early versions of Notepad offered only the most basic functions, such as finding text. Newer versions of Windows include an updated version of Notepad with a search and replace function (Ctrl+H,) as well as (Ctrl+F) for search and similar keyboard shortcuts. Up to Windows, (Fixedsys) was the only available font for Notepad. Windows NT 4.0 and 98 introduced the ability to change this font. In Windows 2000 the default font was changed to Lucida Console.

TO START NOTEPAD

1. Click the Start button, highlight Programs menu item and choose Accessories

2. From the Accessories group, click notepad.

3. To open a new file in the Notepad open the file menu and choose New

4. To open an existing file, open the File menu and choose Open command. In the Open dialog box specify the name and location of the file you want ot open. Click ok. Notepad can open files with the extensions. BAT, .SYS, .INI, & .TXT as these files are all in ASCII code.

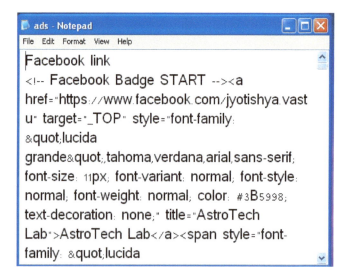

Fig. : NotePad Window

Learn Windows

Note pad application consist of five menu as below

1) File Menu

2) Edit Menu

3) Format Menu

4) View Menu

5) Help Menu

File Menu has following sub-menu as under

1) New   :   This menu use to create a new document. Firstly,   Document creates as untilled name.

2) Open   :   This menu use to open existing documents from the disk.

3) Save   :   This menu use to save a file in disk.

4) Save as   :   This menu use to save a file with other name.

5) Page Setup : This menu use to setup a page

6) Print : This menu use to print a document as a hard copy.

7) Exit : This menu use to close the notepad

Edit Menu has following sub-menu as under

1) Undo : This menu use to retake a action

2) Cut : This menu use to cut the data of file

3) Copy : This menu use to copy a file data to reprint it again.

4) Paste : This menu activated when we click on copy or cut option. Paste menu reprint the copied matters

5) Delete : This menu use to delete the data from file.

6) Find : This menu use to find the data this menu finds particular data from the page of notepad. E.g. If we want to find the word 'Computer' the web search it with the help of his menu

7) Find Next : When we need to find the particular word from the page then we use find and find next to find the same word from all data. e.g. If we want to find how many number of word 'computer' in on page data then we can use this command.

8) Replace : When we want, replace some text from another then we can use this. E.g. when we find the word 'computer' and want to replace it with the new word 'system' then we use this menu.

9) Go To : This menu use to move the cursor to particular line.

10) Select All : This menu use to select the all data at once.

11) Time/Date : This menu print the current date and time on the page.

Format menu has following sub-menu as under

1) Word Wrap : Word wrap is the facility provided by the notepad as margin setting. When we use the word wrap on then text will move to next line automatically.

2) Font   :   This menu use to select the font for writing purpose in notepad.

View menu has following sub-menu as under

1) Status bar   :   This menu is use to ON/OFF the status bar. Status bar contain the line number and columns position of writing the text.

Help menu content the help about the notepad. There is information about notepad how to operate.

MS-PAINT

Paint (formerly Paintbrush for Windows) is a simple graphics-painting program that has been included with almost all versions of Microsoft Windows since its first release. It often referred to as MS Paint or

Microsoft Paint. The program opens and saves files as Windows bitmap (24-bit, 256 color, 16 color, and monochrome, all with the .bmp extension), JPEG, GIF (without animation or transparency).

With the help of this program, we can draw diagrams and picture. We can color the image, cut, and paste the image. This program makes a bitmap file which is useful to export to any application whenever needed. This is very simple drawing application in windows operating system.

TO START PAINT PROGRAM

1. Click the Start button, highlight Programs, choose Accessories

2. From the Accessories group Click Paint.

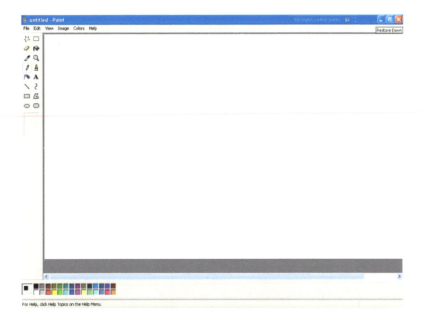

Fig: MS-Paint Window

FEATURES

Recent versions of Paint allow the user to pick up to three colors at a time: the primary color (left mouse click), secondary color (right mouse click), and tertiary color (control key + any mouse click).

The program comes with the following options in its Tool Box :

• **Free-Form Select**

This tool used to select the data of the canvas of paintbrush, as we like freely in form of non-rectangle format.

• **Select**

This tool used to select the data of the canvas of paintbrush in rectangle format only.

• **Eraser/Color Eraser**

This tool used to remove the data of the canvas.

• **Fill with Color**

This tool used to fill any color for the color box provided in the paintbrush application.

• **Pick Color**

This tool used to pick the color from the image. When we select this tool and click on the image color that color ready used in picture.

• Magnifier

This tool used to view the picture in large and small format.

• Pencil

This tool used to draw the picture on the canvas of paintbrush. It works just as manual drawing pencil, which used by the painter for rough sketch. To draw a freeform line in the toolbox, click line. Drag the pointer to draw the line.

Remember

✓ *When you drag the pointer, the foreground color is used. To use the background color holds down the right mouse button and drag the pointer.*

• Brush

This tool used to make the picture more attractive with brushing the picture.

• Airbrush

This tool used to sprinkle the color in the form of dots.

• Text

This tool used to write the textual matter. To type and format text you can only enter text into an image when you are in normal view. To display the normal view, on the View menu, point to Zoom, and then click Normal size.

In the toolbox, click Text to create a text frame, drag the pointer diagonally to the size you want. On the text toolbar, click the font, size, and style you want for the text. If the text toolbar not displayed, on the View menu, click Text Toolbar. You can drag the toolbar to any location in the window. Type your text. You can also paste text into a text box, but not graphics. Text color defined by the foreground color to make the background of the text transparent, click to make the background opaque and defined by the background color click

Remember

✓ *You can enter text in a text box only once. When you click outside the box, the text converted to a graphic image and you cannot make it active again.*

✓ *To change the color of the text, click a color in the color box.*

✓ *To undo up to three changes, on the Edit menu, click Undo for each change.*

• **Line**

This tool used to draw the straight line on canvas. To draw a straight line in the toolbox, click Line.

Below the toolbox, click a line width. Drag the pointer to draw the line.

Remember

✓ *You can draw a perfectly horizontal, vertical, or 45-degree diagonal line by holding down SHIFT while dragging.*

✓ *When you drag the pointer, the foreground color is used. To use the background color, hold down the right mouse button and drag the pointer.*

• Curve

This tool used to draw the curve line on canvas. To draw a curved line in the toolbox, click Curve Below the toolbox, click a line width. Draw a straight line by drawing the pointer. Click where you want one arc of the curve to be, and then drag the pointer to adjust the curve. Repeat this step for a second arc. You can only create two curves for each line.

• Rectangle

This tool used to draw the rectangle on the canvas.

• Polygon

This tool used to draw the polygon on the canvas. To draw a polygon in the toolbox, click Polygon Below the toolbox, click a fill style. Drag the pointer to draw a straight line. Click once at each position where you want a new line segment to appear. Double-click when done.

• Ellipse

This tool used to draw the ellipse on the canvas to draw an ellipse or circle. In the toolbox, click on

Ellipse Below the toolbox, click a fill style. Drag the pointer to draw the ellipse or circle.

• Rounded Rectangle

This tool used to draw the rounded rectangle on the canvas. To draw a rectangle or square In the toolbox, click Rectangle to create a square-cornered shape, or click Rounded Rectangle to create a round-cornered shape. Below the toolbox, click a fill style. To draw a rectangle, drag the pointer diagonally in the direction you want. To draw a square, hold down SHIFT while dragging the pointer.

CALCULATOR

Microsoft Calculator is a calculation application for Microsoft Windows. Many recently made "multimedia keyboards" has a specialized "Calculator" key, which launches Calculator by default. Calculator, despite its simple interface and small size, can perform all of the functions of most four-function or scientific calculators. By default, the application is in the Standard mode, and functions as a four-function calculator. Scientific mode can enabled from the View menu. More advanced functions are available in scientific mode, including logarithms, numerical base conversions, some logical operators, radian, degree and gradients support as well as simple single-variable statistical functions.

You can use Calculator to perform any of the standard operations for which you would normally use a handheld calculator. Calculator performs basic arithmetic, such as addition and subtraction, as well as functions found on a scientific calculator, such as logarithms and factorials.

However, it offers no support for user-defined functions or complex numbers, no storage variables for intermediate results (other than the classic accumulator memory of pocket calculators), no automated polar-Cartesian coordinates conversion and lack of support for two-variables statistics, making it hard or impractical to use with many common simple engineering, physics or even high school tasks, despite its common functions.

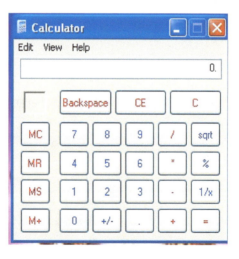

Fig : Calculator

TO USE THE CALCULATOR

1. Click the start button, highlight programs, select Accessories and choose calculator

2. The Calculator program opens in Standard view. To use the Scientific Calculator, open the View menu and choose Scientific.

TO DO A SIMPLE CALCULATION

❖ Type the first number in the calculation.

❖ Click **+** to add, **-** to subtract, ***** to multiply, or **/** to divide.

❖ Type the next number in the calculation.

❖ Type any remaining operators and numbers Click **=** (Equal Sign).

TO DO A SCIENTIFIC CALCULATION

❖ On the **View** menu, click **Scientific**.

❖ Click a number system.

❖ Click the display size you want to use, and then continue with your calculation.

TO DO A STATISTICAL CALCULATION

❖ On the **View** menu, click **Scientific**.

❖ Type your first piece of data, and then click **Sta** to open the **Statistics Box**.

❖ Click **RET** to return to Calculator, and then click **Dat** to save the value.

❖ Type the rest of the data, clicking **Dat** after each entry.

❖ Click **Ave**, **Sum**, or **s**.

TO TRANSFER NUMBERS BETWEEN STANDARD AND SCIENTIFIC VIEW

❖ Click **MS** to store the displayed number.

❖ On the **View** menu, click the desired view.

❖ Click **MR** to recall the stored number.

TO WORK WITH NUMBERS STORED IN MEMORY

❖ To store the displayed number, click **MS**.

❖ To recall a stored number, click **MR**.

❖ To clear the memory, click **MC**.

❖ To add the displayed number to the number already in memory, click **M+**. To see the new number, click **MR**.

TO CONVERT A VALUE TO ANOTHER NUMBER SYSTEM

❖ On the **View** menu, click **Scientific**.

❖ Type the number you want to convert.

❖ Click the number system you want to convert to.

❖ Click to display size you want to use.

WORDPAD

WordPad is a simple word processor that is included with almost all versions of Microsoft Windows from Windows upwards. It more advanced than Notepad, which is rather a basic text editor, but not at al as advanced as Microsoft Word. It originated in Windows 1.0x as Write.

If has facilities to format and printed text, but lacks intermediate features such as a spell checker, thesaurus, support for tables etc. As such, it is suitable for writing letters or short authorships, but underpowered for such tasks as long reports (which usually rely heavily on graphics) or large authorships, such as books or manuscripts.

WordPad introduced for the first time in Windows, replacing the Windows Write application, which came bundled with all previous versions of Windows (version 3.1 and earlier).

To date, WordPad is the only officially supported Microsoft application (apart from Microsoft Word) that can read (or import) the WRI files produced by Windows Write. However, it cannot save files in the WRI format.

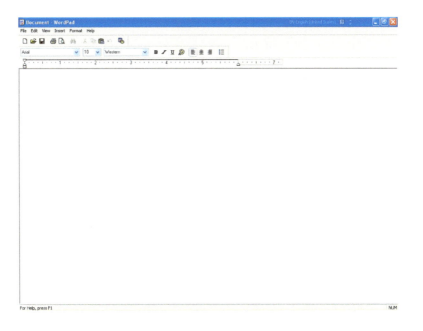

Fig : Wordpad window

TO START WORD PAD

1. Click the Start Button, highlight Programs menu and choose Accessories.

2. From Accessories group, select WordPad

TO OPEN A DOCUMENT

1. Click the File menu and choose Open or press Ctrl + O

2. In the open dialog box choose the name location and type the name of the file, which you want to open.

TO SAVE A DOCUMENTS

1. To name a document or when saving it for the first time click the File menu and choose Save as.

2. To save an existing document open the file menu and choose save or click the save icon on the toolbar.

3.

TO CUT, COPY, PASTE, OR DELETE TEXT

1. To cut text so you can move it to another location, select the text, and then on the **Edit** menu, click **Cut**.

2. To copy text so you can paste it in another location, select the text, and then on the **Edit** menu, click **Copy**.

3. To paste text you have cut or copied, click in the document where you want to paste the   text, and then on the **Edit** menu, click **Paste**.

4. To delete text, select it, and then on the **Edit** menu, click **Clear**.

Remember

✓ *You can select all text at once by clicking **Edit**, and then clicking **Select All**.*

✓ *You can undo your action by clicking **Edit**, and then clicking **Undo**.*

TO CREATE A BULLETED LIST

1. Click where you want the bulleted list to start.

2. On the **Format** menu, click **Bullet Style**, and then type your text. When you press ENTER, another bullet appears on the next line.

3. To end the bulleted list, on the **Format** menu, click **Bullet Style** again.

Remember

✓ *To create an indented paragraph in a bulleted list, press SHIFT+ENTER.*

✓ *You can also create a bulleted list by clicking the **Bullets** button on the format bar.*

TO WRAP TEXT TO THE WINDOW SIZE

1. On the **View** menu, click **Options**.

2. Under **Word wrap**, click the option you want.

Remember

✓ *The wrapping options affect only how text appears on your screen. When printed, the document uses the margin settings specified in* **Page Setup***.*

✓ *You can set different word wrap options for each of the text formats in which you can save documents.*

TO CHANGE A FONT TYPE, STYLE, OR SIZE

❖ Select the text that you want to change.

❖ On the **Format** menu, click **Font**.

❖ Click the options you want.

Remember

✓ *You can specify the font for new text by changing the font settings before you begin to type.*

✓ *You can select all text at once by clicking **Edit**, and then clicking **Select All**.*

TO INDENT A PARAGRAPH

❖ Click anywhere in the paragraph you want to format.

❖ On the **Format** menu, click **Paragraph**.

❖ Under **Indentation**, type a measurement of how far to indent the paragraph.

TO CHANGE THE ALIGNMENT OF A PARAGRAPH

❖ Click anywhere in the paragraph you want to format.

❖ On the **Format** menu, click **Paragraph**.

❖ In **Alignment**, click a position.

TO SET OR REMOVE TAB STOPS IN PARAGRAPHS

❖ Select the paragraphs for which you want to set tab stops.

❖ On the **Format** menu, click **Tabs**.

❖ In the **Tabs** dialog box, do the following:

❖ To set a tab stop, type the measurement for a new tab stop in **Tab stop position**, and then click **Set**.

❖ To delete a tab stop, click it in the list, and then click **Clear**.

❖ To delete all tab stops in the selected paragraph, click **Clear All**.

Remember

✓ *You can also set tab stops by clicking the ruler where you want to set them. To delete tab stops, drag them off the ruler.*

✓ *To change the unit of measurement to inches, centimeters, points, or picas, on the **View** menu, click **Options**, click the **Options** tab, and then click the unit of measurement you want.*

TO PRINT A WORDPAD DOCUMENT

❖ On the **File** menu, click **Print**.

❖ On the **General** tab, select the printer and Preferences you want, and then click **Print**.

TO CHANGE THE APPEARANCE OF A WORDPAD DOCUMENT

❖ On the **File** menu, click **Page Setup**.

❖ In the **Page Setup** dialog box, do any of the following:

❖ To change the paper or envelope size, click a size in **Size**.

❖ To change the paper source, click a tray name or a feeder in **Source**.

❖ To print the document vertically, click **Portrait**; to print the document horizontally, click **Landscape**.

❖ To change the margins, type a value in any of the **Margins** boxes.

❖ To change your printer settings, click **Printer**.

LINKING / EMBEDING WITH WORDPAD

❖ You can use linking and embedding to exchange information between documents created in different programs.

❖ 'Embedding' means inserting information, such as text or a graphic, into another document in another program. The embedded information, or objects, becomes part of the new document. To edit an embedded object, double-click it; the program in which the object created opens. When you finish editing the object and return to your document, the document reflects all of the changes you have made; but the original object remains unchanged. To embed information, use **Copy** and **Paste** on the **Edit** menu.

❖ Linking means inserting information, such as spreadsheet data, that retains a connection to the information stored in another file. Use linking when you want the information updated dynamically as the data in the source file changes.

To link selected information, use **Copy** and **Paste Special**. Some programs do not support linking. If linking is not available, **Paste Special** does not appear on the **Edit** menu.

❖ Use embedding when you want to edit the information separately from the source file or if you think, the source file will be unavailable.

To embed or link an object into WordPad

❖ On the **Insert** menu, click **Object**.

❖ Click **Create from File** and then type or browse to the path and file name in **File**. To embed or link the object, do one of the following:

❖ To embed the object, make sure the **Link** check box cleared.

❖ To link the object, select the **Link** check box.

Remember

✓ *You can also embed or link an object from another document using **Copy** and **Paste** or **Copy** and **Paste Special**, respectively.*

✓ *To create a new object, click **Create New**, and then click an object type. When you are finishing the object creation, click outside the object to return to WordPad.*

TO EDIT LINKED OBJECTS

❖ Click the object to select it.

❖ On the **Edit** menu, point to the type of object you have selected (for example, **Midi Sequence Object** or **Bitmap Image Object**), and then do one of the following:

❖ To modify the object within the WordPad window, click **Edit** or **Edit Package**. When you are finished, click outside the object to return to the WordPad document.

❖ To modify the object in the program in which it created, click **Open** or **Activate Contents**. When you are finished, click **File**, and then click **Exit** to return to the WordPad document.

CREATING SHORTCUTS

What is a desktop shortcut ?

A desktop shortcut, usually represented by an icon, is a small file that points to a program, folder, document, or Internet location. Clicking on a shortcut icon takes you directly to the object to which the shortcut points. Shortcut icons contain a small arrow in

their lower left corner. Shortcuts are merely pointers –
deleting a shortcut will not delete the item to which the
shortcut points.

How to create a desktop shortcut ?

To create a shortcut to an item located on
the Start menu :

1.   Click on Start. The Start menu will appear.

2.   Locate the item to which you want to create a
      shortcut. If the item is located on a submenu, go
      to the submenu.

3.   Right-click and drag the item to your desktop

**To create a shortcut to items visible to
windows explorer.**

1.   Open Windows Explorer.

2.   Minimize the Windows Explorer windows.

3. Locate in Windows Explorer the item to which you want to create a shortcut.

4. Hold down the right mouse button and drag the item onto the desktop..

5. Release the right mouse button. A context menu will appear.

6. Click on Create Shortcut(s) here.

How to rename a desktop shortcut ?

To rename a shortcut

1. Right-Click on the shortcut

2. Click on Rename

3. Type the new name.

How to delete a desktop shortcut ?

To delete a shortcut

1. Click on the shortcut.

2. Press the delete key.

How to change the icon associated with an object?

To change the icon associated with an object

1. Right-click on the icon. The context menu will appear.

2. Click on Properties.

3. Click on the Change Icon button.

4. Click on the icon of your choice.

5. Click on OK.

WINDOWS EXPLORER

Windows Explorer displays the hierarchical structure of files, folders, and drive on your computer. It also shows any network drives that have mapped to drive letters on your computer. You can copy, move, rename, and search for files and folders. For example, you can open a folder that contains a file you want to copy or move, and then drag the file to another folder or drive.

There are other places in where you can view and work with files and folders. My Documents is a convenient place to store documents, graphics, or other files you want to access quickly. You can also view My Network Places, which lists other computers that connected to your Local Area Network (LAN). When you delete files or folders from your hard disk, places them in the Recycle Bin, where you can retrieve them, until you empty the Recycle Bin. Files or folders deleted from a floppy disk or a network drive permanently deleted and not sent to the Recycle Bin.

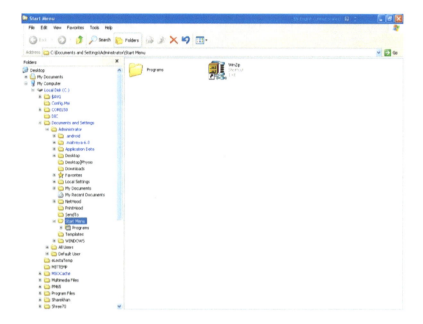

Fig : Windows Explorer

TO SEE THE HIERARCHY OF FOLDERS

Click the Start button, point to Programs and then click Windows Explorer.

Another way to open Windows Explorer is to use the right mouse button to click the 'My computer' icon, and then click Explore to show or hide folders on the left side of the window, click the plus or minus sign beside the folder.

You can organize the file and folders by using the 'My computer' and Windows Explorer.

MOVING AND COPING A FILE OR FOLDER

1. Double-click the 'My computer'. Find the file or folder you want to move or copy and then click it.

2. Click Edit. To move the file, Click Cut. To make a copy of the file, Click copy.

3. Open the folder where you want to place the file, click Edit the then Paste.

A quick way to move and copy files and folders is to use right mouse button.

DELETING A FILE OR FOLDER

1.   Double-click My computer. Find the file or folder you want to delete and then click it.

2.   On the file menu, click Delete.

CREATING A NEW FOLDER

1.   Double-click My Computer and then double-click the disk drive or folder in which you want   to place the new folder.

2.   Click on the File menu, point to New and then Click Folder.

3.   Type the name of the new folder and press Enter.

COPYING A FILE TO FLOPPY DISK

1.   Double-click My computer. Find the file or folder you want to copy and then click it.

2. On the File menu, point to Sent To and then click the drive where you want to copy the file or folder.

STARTING AND QUITTING A PROGRAM

1. Click the Start Program and then point to programs

2. Point to the folder, such as Accessories that contains the program and then click the program. E.g. To start paint application, click on start -> programs -> accessories - > paint

TO QUIT THE PROGRAM

Click the Close button in the upper-right corner of the windows

As shown in above figure Windows Explorer window will appear. Windows separates the window into two panes. If you click on an object in the left pane, the contents of the object displays in the right pane. Click on Desktop and the contents of the Desktop folder display on the right. Click on My computer and your computer resources display on the right. To see the contents of a drive, click on the drive. To see the contents of a folder, click on the icon for the folder in the left pane.

TO CREATE A NEW FOLDER

1. In the left pane, click on the drive or folder in which you want to create the new folder.

2. Click on any free area in the right pane. A context menu will appear.

3. Highlight New.

4. Click on Folder

5. Type in a name for the folder.

WINDOWS EXPLORER VIEWS

Windows Explorer provides you with the following choices: large Icons, Small icons, list, and details, large icons and Small Icons, as their names imply, determine the size of the icon. List displays all of the files and folders without supplying the size, type, or date modified. Details display the size, type, and date modified. To change the view:

1. Right-click on any free area in the right pane.

    A context menu will appear.

2. Highlight View.

3. Select the view you want from the drop-down menu.

TO DELETE A FILE OR FOLDER

1. Right-click on the file or folder you want to delete. A context menu will appear.

2. Click on Delete. Window Explorer will ask, "Are you sure want to send this object to the recycle bin ?"

3. Click on "Yes".

TO COPY A FILE OR FOLDER

1. Right-click on the file or folder you want to copy. A context menu will appear

2. Click on Copy. The file or folder should now be on the clipboard.

TO CUT A FILE OR FOLDER

1. Right-click on the file or folder you want to cut. A context menu will appear.

2. Click on cut. The file or folder should now be on the clipboard.

TO PASTE A FILE OR FOLDER

1. After cutting or copying the file, right-click on the object or in the right pane of the folder to which you want to paste. A context menu will appear.

2. Type the new name.

CONTROL PANEL

In recent versions of Windows, the Control Panel has two views, Classic view and Category View, and it is possible to switch between these through an option that appears on the left side of the windows.

Control Panel is a part of the Microsoft Windows graphical user interface which allows users to view and manipulate basic system settings and controls, such as adding hardware, adding and removing software, controlling user accounts, and changing accessibility options. Additional applets can provide by third party software.

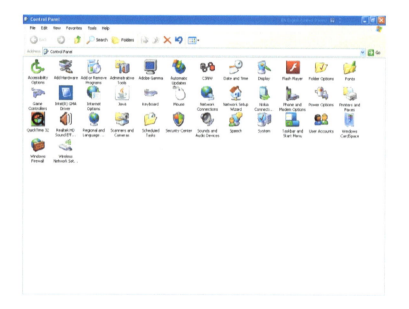

fig : Classic View of Control Panel

List of Control Panel applets (Windows)

Accessibility Options allows users to configure the accessibility of their PC. It comprises various settings primarily aimed at users with disabilities or hardware problems.

❖ The behavior of the keyboard can modified, this aimed at people who have difficulty pressing key-combinations, or pressing a key just once.

❖ Behavior of sounds can modify.

❖ High contrast mode can activate.

❖ The keyboard cursor can customize.

❖ The mouse pointer can controlled using the keyboard.

ADD NEW HARDWARE

Launched wizard allows users to add new hardware devices to the system. This can do by selecting from a list of devices or by specifying the location of the driver installation files.

ADD OR REMOVE PROGRAMS

The Add/Remove Programs dialog allows the user to manipulate software installed on the system in a number of ways:

❖ Allows users to uninstall and change existing software packages, as well as indicating how much space individual programs take and how frequently they are used.

❖ Allows users to manually install software from an CD-ROM or Floppy Disk, and install add-ons from Windows Update.

❖ Allows users to change which Windows components are install, via the Windows setup Wizard, which includes Internet Explorer, Window Media Player and Windows Messenger.

❖ Finally, it allows user to specify the default applications tasks, via the set program access and defaults wizard, such as internet browsers, media players and email programs and whether access to these programs is available.

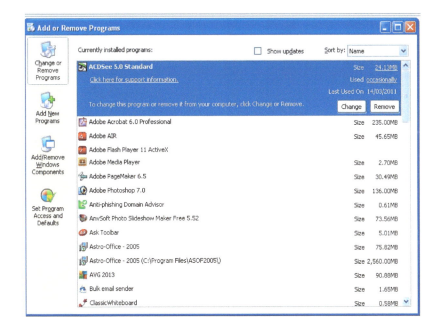

Fig : Add Remove program window

DATE AND TIME

Allows user to change the date and time stored in the machines BIOS, change the time zone and specify whether to synchronize the date and time with an Internet Time Server and which server to use. Display

❖ Allows users to change the desktop background (wallpaper) to a picture of their choice and specifies how it should show.

❖ Allows the user to change or disable the screensaver, and specify how long it takes to activate and whether to ask for a password on resume.

❖ Allows the user to specify the color styles of all elements within the system, primarily whether to use the Windows / Vista styles (blue by default in XP) or to use the classic Windows/Me styles, this also allows the user to change the My computer and Recycle Bin icons.

❖ Allows the user to change the screen resolution and color quality, and provides troubleshooting advice for displays.

KEYBOARD

Let us the user change and test keyboard settings, including cursor blink rate and key repeat rate.

MOUSE

Mouse allows the configuration of pointer options, such as the double click and scroll speed, and include visibility options such as whether to leave trails behind the mouse pointer and whether the pointer should disappear when typing. This also allows the user to specify the pointer appearance for each task, such as resize and busy.

MY COMPUTER

My computer icon lets you browse through all the resources attached to your PC. When you click on 'My Computer' icon, It shows in the figure below.

It is use to see the computer storage drive data of system. This window includes icons of each of the computer's disk drives (floppy disk, hard disk, CD-ROM, Zip drive etc. and network directories if you have connected your PC to a network. It also shows additional system folders, providing access to the Windows Control Panel, Printers, Dial-up networking, and a folder that manages scheduled tasks.

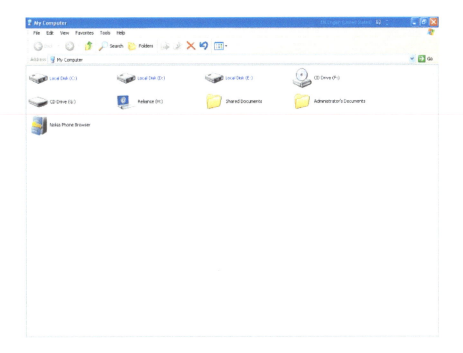

Fig : My Computer Window

MY DOCUMENTS

On Microsoft Windows operating systems, My documents is the name of a special folder on the computer's hard drive that is commonly used to store a user's documents music, pictures, downloads, and other files.

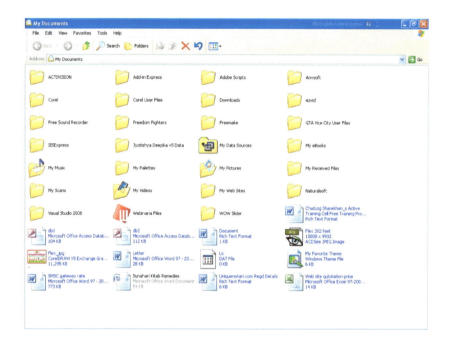

Fig : My Document Window

RECYCLE BIN

The Recycle Bin provides a safety net when deleting files or folders. When you delete any of these items from your hard disk, Windows places it in the Recycle Bin and the Recycle Bin icon changes from empty to full. Items deleted from a floppy disk or a network drive permanently deleted and not forwarded to the Recycle Bin.

Items in the Recycle Bin remain there until you decide to delete permanently them from your computer. These items still take up hard disk space and can be undeleted or restored back to their original location. When it fills up, Windows automatically cleans out enough space in the Recycle Bin to accommodate the most recently deleted files and folders.

If you are running low on hard disk space, always remember to empty the Recycle Bin. You can also restrict the size of the Recycle Bin to limit the amount of hard disk space it takes up.

Windows allocates one Recycle Bin for each partition or hard disk. If your hard disk partitioned, or if you have more than one hard disk in your computer, you can specify a different size for each Recycle Bin.

To empty the Recycle Bin

1.   On the desktop, double-click Recycle Bin

2.   On the File menu, Click Empty Recycle Bin.

Finding files or folders

If you do not know where the document or folder is, you can use the find command to find and open it.

To find something

1.   Click the start button and then point to find.

2.   Click Files or folders.

3.   Click the Names box and then type name of the file or folder, which you want to find.

4.   To specify find where to search, click the arrow next to the Look in Box or click Browse.

5.   To start the search, click Find Now.

Changing System Settings

To change the date and / or time

1.   Click on the Start button, which is located in the lower left corner of the screen. The Start menu will appear.

2.   Highlight Settings. A Submenu will appear.

3.   Click on Control Panel. The Control Panel will open.

4.   Click on Date / Time. The Date / Time Properties dialog box will appear.

5.   In the Date frame, select the month and year.

6.   In the month field, click to open the drop-down menu and select the current month.

7. Type the year in the Year field or use the arrows next to the field to move forward or backward until you get to the current year.

8. The Time field divided into four segments: hour, minutes, seconds, and AM and PM. to make an adjustment.

9. Click in the segment and either type in the correct information or use the arrow keys on the right side to select the correct hour, minute, second or AM or PM.

10. Select the correct time zone from the drop-down menu.

11. If you want the clock to adjust automatically to daylight saving time, check the box on the screen.

12. Click on the Apply button.

13. Click on OK.

SCREEN SAVER

Computer monitors display images by firing electron beams at a phosphor-coated screen. If the same image stays on the screen for too long, there is a danger that the image will leave a permanent imprint on the screen. Screen savers help prevent this possibility by providing a constantly changing image.

To select a screen saver

1. Right-click anywhere on the Windows desktop. A menu will appear.

2. Select Active Desktop.

3. Click on Customize My Desktop.

4. Click on the Screen Saver tab.

5. The Screen Saver field provides the list of available screen savers. Select the screen saver you want from the list.

6. Click on Settings to set the display options associated with the screen saver.

7. Click on checkmark 'Password Protected' option to set a password for your screen saver. Password protection prevents the screen saver from turned off unless a password entered.

8. Click on Change to set the password.

9. Set the number of minutes of activity before the screen saver starts in the wait field.

10. Click on OK.

Fig : Screen Saver

WALLPAPER

Wallpaper is the background that displays on your desktop. If you have your desktop set to View as a Web Page, your wallpaper can be an image or an HTML file.

If your desktop is not set to View as a Web page, wallpaper can only be an image.

Fig : Display Property Window to Change the desktop image

To set my desktop to view as a Web Page

Set your desktop to view as a Web Page.

1.   Right-click on your desktop. A menu will appear.

2.   Highlight Active Desktop.

3.   If view as a menu has a checkmark next to it, your desktop already viewed as Web pages. If view as a Web Page does not have a checkmark next to it, click on View as a Web Page.

How do I change my wallpaper ?

To change your wallpaper.

1.   Right-click on your desktop

2.   Highlight Active Desktop.

3.   Click on Customize My desktop.

4.   Click on the Background tab.

5.   Select the wallpaper you want from the list that appears in the Select an HTML Document or Picture Box.

Appearance & Themes

The Appearance & Themes category in the Control Panel contains links to common ways you can customize the appearance of your Windows computer. The common tasks you can perform include

Change the computer's theme Changing the Background of Your Desktop from the Start menu, click on the control Panel icon. To open the Display Tool Once the Control Panel opens, double-click on the Display icon. Select the Desktop Tab after the Display Properties dialog box opens, click on the desktop tab, and Select a Background Under background, Windows provides several pictures and patterns you can choose. Click on one of the pictures or patterns. It will highlight after you have selected it.

Apply Your Changes

Click Apply to see what the picture or pattern looks like on your desktop. It may take a couple seconds for the picture on your desktop to change.

Once you are satisfied with background you have chose, click OK to close the Display Properties dialog box.

Choose a screen saver

Open the Control Panel

Click on start menu, and then click on the Control Panel icon. After the Control Panel opens, double-click on the Display icon Click on the Screen Saver tab.

1. Click on the drop-down menu under Screen Saver to expand it.

2. Click on the screen saver you wish to use. E.g. you can click on 3D Flower Box

3.	Click Preview to see what the screen saver looks like.

4.	Click on OK to select the screen saver.

Change the screen resolution

By changing the screen resolution, you can increase the size or amount of information that can be displayed on the screen at once, but increasing the size decreases the amount of information on the screen and vice versa.

❖	Higher resolution = more information on the screen, but each item is smaller

❖	Lower resolution = bigger items, but less information on the screen

❖	Since increasing the screen, resolution allows you to display more information on the screen at once, it can be a good option when you have more than program open or when you're browsing the Internet.

❖ On the other hand, decreasing the size of items on the screen can be a good option for people who are visually impaired. It can also be useful if you struggle to click on small icons or other elements and want them to appear larger on the screen.

Fig : Display Properties window to change resolution of windows

To change screen resolution in

1. Right-click on a blank area of the desktop and click on Properties.

2. Click on the Settings tab to access the screen resolution setting.

Your Display Properties dialog box will look different from the one pictured above, but look for the screen resolution slider. To increase the screen resolution, move the slider toward more. To decrease screen resolution, move it toward less. When you are finished, click OK to save your changes.

The appearance and Themes category also contains panel icons that link to tools you can use to customize your Windows appearance. The icons include:

❖ Folder Options

❖ Display

Learn Windows

❖ Taskbar and Start Menu

Folder Options

The folder options tools allow you to customize how files and folders display. You can change what program different file types are associated with, make network files available offline, or setup Windows Professional to support more control of folder and file privacy. Below are links to tutorials you can follows to learn how to use the Folder Options tools:

Show the Security Tab in Windows Professional Is your security tab missing. To show the security tab in Windows Professional, you must disable simple file sharing. Once your security tab is visible, you can set, view, change, or remove file and folder permissions in Windows Professional.

To disable simple file sharing and show the security tab in Windows Professional, first click on the Control Panel link in the Start menu.

1.   Click on Appearance and Themes. If you are Control Panel looks different from the one pictured above, you need to switch to the   category   view of the Control Panel.

2.   Click on Folder Options.

3.   The Folder Options dialog box opens. Select the View tab. Under Advanced settings, uncheck the Use simple file sharing [Recommended] box. Save your changes by clicking on OK. When you view the properties of a file or folder in Windows Professional, you'll have a security tab. Use the options on that tab to set, view, change, or remove file and folder permissions.

SYSTEM TOOLS

1. BACKUP

The Backup utility helps you create a copy of the information on your hard disk In the event that the original data on your hard disk is accidentally erased or overwritten, or becomes inaccessible because of a hard disk malfunction; you can use the copy to restore your lost or damaged data.

1. To start Backup, click start, point to All Programs, point to Accessories, point to System tools, and the click Backup

2. The Removable Storage service started for Backup to work properly.

3. You can also use the Automated System Recovery Wizard in the Backup utility to help you repair your system.

2. DISK CLEANUP

Disk Cleanup helps free up space on your hard drive Disk Cleanup searches your drive, and then shows you temporary files, Internet cache files, and unnecessary program files that you can safely delete. You can direct Disk Cleanup to delete some or all of those files.

Open Disk Cleanup

To open Disk Cleanup, click Start, point to All Programs, Point to Accessories, Point to System Tools, and then click Disk Cleanup.

3. DISK DEFRAGMENTER

You might need to be log on as an administrator or a member of the Administrators group in order to perform some tasks.

Disk Defragmenter consolidates fragmented files and folders on your computer's hard disk, so that each occupies a single, contiguous space on the volume As a result, your system can gain access to your files and folders and save new ones more efficiently. By consolidating your files and folders, Disk Defragmenter also consolidates the volume's free space, making it less likely that new files will be fragment. To open Disk Defragmenter, click Start, point to All Programs, point to Accessories, point to System Tools, and then click Disk Defragmenter

4. FILES AND SETTINGS TRANSFER WIZARD

The Files and Settings Transfer Wizard helps you move your data files and personal settings from your old computer to your new one, without having to go through much of the same configuration you did with your old computer. E.g. you can take your personal display properties, folder and taskbar options, and Internet browser and mail settings from your old computer and place them on the new one. The wizard will also move specific files or entire folders, such as My Documents, My Pictures, and Favorites.

Open the Files and Settings Transfer Wizard

To open the Files and Settings Transfer Wizard, Click start, point to All Programs, point to Accessories, point to System Tools, and then click Files and Settings Transfer Wizard.

5. SCHEDULED TASKS OVERVIEW

With Scheduled Tasks, you can schedule any script, program, or document to run at a time that is most convenient for you. Scheduled Tasks starts each time you start Windows and runs in the background.

With Scheduled Tasks, you can also. Schedule a task to run daily, weekly, monthly, or at certain times (such as system startup) Change the schedule for a task. Stop a scheduled task. Customize how a task will run at a scheduled time.

To schedule a new task

1.   Open Scheduled Tasks.

2.   Double-click Add Scheduled Task.

3.   Follow the instructions in the Scheduled Task Wizard.

❖   Confirm that the system date and time on your computer are accurate, because Scheduled Tasks relies on this information to run scheduled tasks.

To verify or change this information, double-click the time indicator on the taskbar.

❖ You must supply the password for the account on which you want the scheduled task to run. The password cannot be blank.

To modify a scheduled task

1. Open Scheduled Tasks.

2. Right-click the task you want to modify, and then click Properties.

3. Do one or more of the following.

❖ To change a program run, in Run, type the path for the new program.

❖ To change the schedule for the task, click the Schedule tab.

❖ To customize the settings for the task, such as maximum run time, idle time requirements, and power management options, click the Settings Tab.

❖ To set security for the task, click the Security tab.

6. CHARACTER MAP

You can use Character Map to copy and paste special characters into your documents, such as the trademark symbol, special mathematical character from the character set of another language.

Open Character Map

To open Character Map, Click Start, point to All Programs, point to Accessories, point to System Tools, and then click Character Map.

Special Characters

When creating your documents, you may need to use a special character in your text, such as a trademark or degree symbol. To see all the characters you can use for a particular font, click Start, point to All Programs, point to Accessories, point to System Tools, and then Click Character Map. You can copy and paste the characters you need from Character Map into your document.

If the character you need not displayed in Character Map, you can design your own character using Private Character Editor (PCE). Using PCE, you can draw special letters, logos, or ideographs, and link them into your font library for repeated use.

7. SYSTEM INFORMATION

System Information collects and displays your system configuration information. Support technicians require specific information about your computer so they can resolve your system problem. You can use System Information to find quickly the data they need.

Open System Information

To open System Information, click Start, and then click Run. In the Open box, type msinfo32.exe.

8. SYSTEM RESTORE OVERVIEW

System Restore is a component of Windows Professional that you can use to restore your computer to a previous state, if a problem occurs, without losing your personal data files (such as Microsoft Word documents, browsing history, drawings, favorites, or email). System Restore monitors changes to the system and some application files, and it automatically creates easily identified restore points. These restore points allow you to revert the system to a previous time. They created daily and at the time of significant system events (such as when an application or driver installed). You can also create and name your own restore points at any time.

9. SECURITY CENTER

Security Center is a new service in Windows, which provides a central location for changing security settings, learning more about security, and helping to ensure that the user's computer is up to date. You can use Security Center by double-clicking the Security

Center icon in Control Panel or selecting Start - > Programs - > Accessories - > Security Center.

The Security Center Service runs as a background process and checks the state of the following components on the user's computer.

10. FIREWALL

The Security Center Checks whether Windows Firewall is ON / OFF. It also check for the presence of some other software firewalls by querying for specific WMI providers made available by participating vendors.

11. VIRUS PROTECTION

The Security center checks for the present of antivirus software using queries for specific WMI providers that made available by participating vendors. If the information is available, the Security Center service also determines whether the software is up-to-date and whether real-time scanning turned on.

12. AUTOMATIC UPDATES

The Security Center checks to make sure that Automatic Updates set to the recommended setting, which automatically downloads and installs critical updates to the user's computer. If Automatic Updates is turn off or is not set to the recommended settings, the Security Center provides appropriate recommendations.

If a component is found to be missing or out of compliance with your security policy, the Security Center places a red icon in the notification area of the users taskbar and provides an Alert message at logon. This message contains links to open the Security Center user interface, which displays a message about the problem and provides recommendations for fixing it.

In case where users are running firewall or antivirus software that not detected by Security Center, the user has the option to set the Security Center to bypass alerting for that component.

In Control Panel, Security Center also serves as a starting point for Control Panel items related to security and security-related Web links.

Starting a Program using RUN command

If you know the name and path of the program you want to run, you can use the Run command to start it easily.

To start a program or open a folder or a document, do the following:

1. Click the Start Button and then click Run.

2. Type the name of the program, folder or document you want to open. Alternatively, click the Browser to look for the item.

    When you use the Run command, you can often specify just the name of the program instead of the full path.

    A path is a more direct way to describe where the file, such as a document or program is located on your computer or the network. It lists the drive, such as the hard disk, floppy disk, CD-ROM drive or shared network folder that contains the document. It also lists all the folders that you need to open to find the document.

    To specify the full path of for a document, type the drive letter, followed by a colon (:) and backslash (\). Then list the folders in the order you open them. If there is more than one, separate the names by backslashes. Then type the filename.

Example: to specify the location of the readme file, which is located on drive C in the Windows folder, you would type:

C:\Windows\readme.txt

SETTING PERIPHERALS

Setting up a Printer

Setting up your printer is easy and fast, using Add Printer Wizard, as systematic printer setup programs.

Before you begin, make sure your printer correctly connected to your computer and that you know the make and model of the printer. If you are planning to use a shared printer over the network, you may also need to know the path to it. Or you can browse for the printer in Network Neighborhood and then double-click its icon to set it up.

To set up a printer for use with Windows

1. Click the start button, point to settings and click printers.

2. Double-click Add printer

3. Follow the instructions on your screen.

Printing a document

After you have set up a printer, you can easily print your document. To print your document, if the document is open, click File and then click Print.

INSTALLING SOFTWARE

Windows provide a quick way to set up new programs on your computer.

To install programs

1. Click the Start button, point to Setting and then click Control Panel.

2. You can add or remove components of Windows by clicking the Windows Setup tab in the Add/remove Program Window.

3. Double click Add/Remove programs.

4. Follow the instruction on your screen

INSTALING HARDWARE

Windows can help you set up new hardware, such as a sound card on your system. If you have not already inserted you hardware card in your computer, you should do so before starting this procedure. You should turn off and unplug your computer before taking the cover off.

DRIVERS

Drivers are a program, which controls a device. Every device, whether it is a printer, disk drive, or keyboard, must have a driver program. Many drivers, such as the keyboard driver, come with the operating system. For other devices, you may need to load a new driver when you connect the device to your computer. In DOS systems, drivers are files with SYS extension. In Windows environments, drivers often have DRV extension.

A driver acts like a translator between the device and programs that use the device. Each device has its own set of specialized commands only its driver knows. In contrast, most programs access devices by using generic commands. The driver, therefore, accepts generic commands from a program and then translates them into specialized commands for the device.

NEW FEATURES IN WINDOWS VERSION

Active Desktop

Windows desktop acts a little differently than the old. The Windows beta incorporates the Active Desktop to make you desk come alive with active content, such as weather maps that automatically update using the Internet. What more than just a weather map ? How about stock tickers, up-to-date headline, news or the latest sports scores ? These are just come of the many possibilities for your active desktop-you choose what you want on your Active Desktop.

Task Scheduler

When was the last time you look out the extra garbage on your hard disk that's slowing down your computer ? If you are a little behind at taking care of some of the maintenance chores that keep your PC running at top efficiently. There are lots of little things people forget to do and taking the time to maintain your PC probably isn't at the top of your list. How would you like a little help ?

The Windows has a nifty built-in feature that you only got with Windows if you spend extra to buy the Plus! Add-in the Task Scheduler. The Task Scheduler helps you out by making sure all those little maintenance tasks done for you.

New Utilities

The most important new utilities in the Windows include the System information Utility, the System File Checker and the Windows Tune Up Wizard.

TV Viewer

With TV viewer, you can view local television schedules, search for particular shows, have your PC remind you when your favorite show will be on and with the right equipment.

Imaging

The Windows includes Imaging, a new graphics program created by Kodak, Which promises to help you view, print and annotate nearly any type of PC-based image file. This may not sound too exciting, but when was the last time you tried to add some notes to a fax someone sent to your PC ? Imaging make easy !

FEATURES OF WINDOWS

Windows introduced several new features to the Windows line, including

❖ Faster start-up and hibernation sequences

❖ The ability to discard a newer device driver in favors of the previous one (known as driver rollback), should a driver upgrade not produce desirable results.

❖ This includes the framework to develop themes for the desktop environment.

❖ It is fast user switching, which allows a user to save the current state, open applications of their desktop, and allow another user to log on without losing that information.

❖ Clear Type font rendering mechanism, which designed to improve text readability on Liquid Crystal Display (LCD) and similar monitors.

❖ Remote Desktop functionality allows users to connect to a computer running Windows from across a network or the Internet and access their applications, files, printers, and devices.

❖ Support for most DSL modems and wireless network connections, as well as networking over FireWire.

FEATURES OF VISTA VERSIONS

1. Easier

Windows Vista makes it faster and easier than ever to find, use, manage, share, and enjoy information – on your PC and on the web.

Make a smooth transition to Windows Vista : Windows Easy Transfer simplifies the process of setting up your new PC by automatically transferring your important items – including files, folders, photos, music, settings, and e-mail messages –from your old computer to your new one.

Organize a lifetime of photos and movies with ease using Windows Photo Gallery. Tag your photos by date, keyword, star rating, or any identifying label you want – so you can find them when you want them. When you're ready to print, select your best photos and easily send them to your favorite location to be printed with Online Printing on Windows Vista.

2. Find, enjoy and share that extra-special shot

Windows Internet Explorer helps your browse the web more efficiently. View multiple web pages simultaneously in one window with tabbed browsing or use Quick Tabs to see thumbnail images of all your open web pages.

3. Another convenient way to surf

Use Windows Sidebar with customizable mini-applications called Gadgets for at-a-glance access to weather, news, calendar, and other useful information.

4. Windows Complete PC Backup and Restore

A complete restore is ideal to recovery. Available in Windows Vista Business, Ultimate, and Enterprise editions, Complete PC Backup and Restore is a comprehensive, image-based backup tool to help you out of a tight spot if you need to recover your entire system. While file restore is useful in cases of file loss and data corruption, Windows Complete PC Restore is most useful for to recovery when your PC malfunctions Complete PC Backup and Restore is capable of restoring your entire PC environment, including the operating system, installed programs, user settings and data files.

You can restore your PC back to its original state, or to a replacement PC. Complete PC Restore initiated from within Windows Vista or from the Windows Vista installation CD in the event the PC is so corrupt that it cannot start up normally from the hard disk.

Some product features are only available in certain editions of Windows Vista and may require advanced or additional hardware.

5. Internet Explorer Dynamic Security Protection

Through a robust new architecture, Internet Explorer offers multiple, interrelated security features to help defend your PC against malware (malicious code or unwanted software, including worms, viruses, adware, and spyware). Among the browser's dynamic security protections are safeguards to help make sure your personal information does not fall into the hands of fraudulent or deceptive websites.

Web browsers perform much function. They must be open and flexible enough to handle a mix of website activity while maintaining sufficiently high security to prevent unwanted data access or application behaviors, managing this balance is a top priority for Microsoft.

Microsoft has two primary security objectives with Internet Explorer

❖ Protection against malware

❖ Personal data safeguards

Protection against malware

Malware, short for malicious software, refers to software applications designed to damage or disrupt a user's system. The proliferation of malware and its impact on security were some of the key driving forces behind the design features of Internet Explorer 7. The new version has improved to reduce the potential for hackers to harm a system by limiting the amount of damage that can do if malware is able to find its way onto a use's system. In addition, Internet Explorer includes several technical features designed to thwart hackers' efforts to trick you into entering personal data when you should not. Core parts of the browser's architecture have also fortified to better defend against exploitation and improve the way the browser handles data.

Protected Mode

Available only to people running Internet Explorer in Windows Vista, Protected Mode provides new levels of security and data protection for Windows users, Designed to defend against "elevation of privilege" attacks, Protected Mode provides the safety of a robust Internet browsing experience while helping prevent hackers from taking over the system and installing programs or deleting your information.

In 'Protected Mode', Internet Explorer in Windows Vista cannot modify user or system activity that tries to put something on your machine or start another program. By ensuring the user consents to these kinds of actions, the likelihood of automated and / or unwanted software installation reduced. This feature also makes you aware of what a website is trying to do, giving you a chance to stop it and take time to check double the trustworthiness of the website.

6.   Parental Controls

Control your children's computer use from one screen. The parental controls built into Windows Vista are designed to put parents' minds at easy and give them confidence in their ability to manage exactly what their children can do on the computer. These controls help parents determine which games their children can play, which programs they can use, and which websites they can visit- and when. Parents can restrict computer use to specific times and trust that Windows Vista will enforce those restrictions, even when they are away from home.

The Parental Controls panel, part of the User Accounts and Family Safety Control Panel applet, centralizes all of the key settings of the Windows Vista Parental Controls from this one location, you can configure the parental controls for your computer and applications, setting appropriate limits on your children's game playing, web browsing, and overall computer use. The Parental Controls panel provides a centralized location where you can turn parental controls on and off; block or allow specific programs, games, and websites, and set controls for every aspect of your child's computer use. Third-party family safety software and services providers may also choose to have their products and services accessible from the Parental Controls panel in Windows Vista. Parental Controls does not work on domain-joined machines, such as in a business environment.

7. Activity reports

From the Parental Control panel, you can review easy-to-read activity reports that show how your children have been using the computer. Monitoring your children's computer behavior not only makes it easy for your to keep track of what they are seeing, hearing, and doing, but it also enables you to refine and modify parental controls based on actual feedback. For your children, the Parental Controls icon in the system tray is always visible to let them know that the Parental Controls features is on.

8. Time limits for computer use

With Windows Vista, you can decide when your children allowed, or not allowed, to use the computer. You presented with a grid showing the days of the week and the hours of the day.

Set time limits for computer use

The default setting is to allow your children to use the computer during all hours of the day and night, seven days a week. To restrict their computer use, you simply click the specific times and days that you want to block. As a child nears the end of an approved time, they receive a 15-minute and a 1-minute notification that their time is about to expire. If their time ends before they log off the computer, Windows Vista suspends their session and displays the logon screen so another user can use the computer. The child's session stays active in the background, however, so the next time they log on, they can pick up where they left off without losing any of their work.

9. Internet Explorer in Windows Vista

Internet Explorer in Windows Vista features a new and cleaner interface.

Windows Internet Explorer in Windows Vista, the new version of the popular web browser represents a major step forward in making everyday web tasks easier.

10. Making everyday tasks easier

To help you perform tasks more productively and efficiently, Internet Explorer has redesigned with new and enhanced capabilities for searching and making use of myriad sources of information.

Everyday tasks are easier with improved navigation through tabbed browsing and web search right from the toolbar. Improved printing and the ability to easily discover, read, and subscribe to Really Simple Syndication (RSS) feeds enable you to access only the information you want, any time it is convenient.

11. Dynamic security protection

Through a robust new architecture, Internet Explorer offers dynamic security protection. It defend against malicious software (also known as malware), as well as new ways to protect users from unintentionally. It is providing personal data to fraudulent websites that use deceptive practices such as phishing And Internet Explorer in Windows Vista. It provides Parental Controls and a Protected Mode setting to keep families safer online and to help protect your PC from web-based attacks.

12. Cleaner, Sleeker user interface

Internet Explore offers a new look to minimize the number of toolbars you need while maximizing the amount of screen space devoted to the WebPages you care about. Internet Explorer is noticeably simpler, more streamlined, and less cluttered. It reduces the toolbar "creep" – consecutive rows of buttons and tools that can sometime take up as much as a third of the screen. Simpler, more streamlined frame. The Back and Forward buttons are now smaller and have moved next to the Address Bar. The Windows flag icon in the upper right corner of Internet Explorer 6 has replaced with the powerful Instant Search field.

13. Efficient for Small Businesses

Getting it done just got easier. With Windows Vista Business, it is easier and faster than ever to find, use, manage, and share the information on your PC, on your server, or on the web. Innovative navigational tools in the Windows Aero user interface make it easier to find and access recently used documents and programs.

Designed specifically for small businesses, the one-click Windows Fax and Scan features in Windows Vista Business make it easy to send and receive faxes, scan documents and images, and share those resources with others.

14. Send and receive faxes via e-mail

Spend less time learning how to manage your computers and more time honing your business. Small business resources in Windows Vista include a guided tour of the operating system with clear instructions and practical, easy-to-use advice.

Tablet PC support in Windows Vista Business helps you enjoy the best in touch technologies: page through files or websites with just a flick of your pen.

Put imagery to work in your business. Easily edit pictures, quickly view thumbnail images, and label pictures with your own tags for quick retrieval using Windows Photo Gallery.

15. Safer for Small Businesses

Your business data is invaluable – and Windows Vista Business comes with advanced. Intuitive data protection and safety features in place, so you can worry less about your data and more about your customers.

On guard at all times, Windows Defender helps protect your company's PCs by regularly scanning them and offering to remove any spyware or other unwanted software that it finds.

16. Always-on-protection

Help protect your information with scheduled backups and recovery tools that can task up entire hard disk drives and easily retrieve previous version of individual documents.

17. Automate your backups

Shadow Copy automatically creates point-in-time copies of files as you work, so you can easily retrieve versions of a document that you may have accidentally deleted or overwritten. Shadow Copy automatically turned on in Windows Vista. On a scheduled basis, it creates copies of files that have changed. Because only incremental changes saved, minimal disk space is use for shadow copies.

18. Hard disk maintenance automated

Windows Vista Business includes a new system-image backup feature that can completely back up an entire PC, including its personal and system files, programs and settings. Unlike previous backup methods, Complete PC Backup and Restore takes a perfect 'picture' of your PC's hard disks, which can be called upon if your entire system ever needs to be restore.

FEATURES OF WINDOWS 10

WINDOWS 10 give tough competition to Google.com. This is as easy as Windows Vista but it has advanced features with this new version of Windows

Operating System. The most important features of this operating system are 'Parental Control'. We can restrict any Website, File, Folder, Video, Games at any time this concept called as 'Parental Control'. This feature is useful to avoid the child from misuse of computer or to introduce unwanted data like proxy site, porn data etc.

1) This operating system takes less time to shutdown the system.

2) We can find the files and folder very fast due to windows search engine facility.

3) This OS give fast browsing facility.

4) We can directly use our favorite website by using Web slice option in Internet Explorer also use a visual preview option and see the website preview.

5) We can send and receive the photo, video songs, and messages with the help of windows essential option in this operating system.

6) We can use our home and office computer from other place by using Remote media streaming option.

7) We can protect our computer from any malicious software by using screen filter option.

IMP QUESTIONS

1. Explain the following:

    i) Control Panel   ii) Windows explorer

2. What are the advantages of Windows/98? Explain the concept of Multi-user and multiprogramming in Windows/98.

3. What are the uses of Run command in Windows/98? Explain how you will install any software's in Windows/98?

4. What is Windows? Explain its features.

5. Explain Windows. State its advantages over Windows

6. What is Windows Explorer? Write down the procedure to find the files and folders.

7. How will you set printers, mouse add display adapter? Explain its procedure.

8. Write a short note on accessories and system tools.

9. Write a short note on :

    i) Games   ii) notepad iii) calculator

10. Write down the procedure of changing system settings in Windows

11. Write down the purpose of the following:

    i) Desktop ii) Control Panel

    iii) Run   iv) Icon

12. Explain various Windows Accessories in details.

13. Write a short note on

    i) My Computer

    ii) My Documents

    iii) Recycle bin

14. Explain various features of Windows/ Vista

15. Explain systematic procedure to find files & folders stored on drive d:

16. Write procedure for creating shortcuts

17. Write short note on Windows explorer.

18. Explain any 5-system tools.

19. How can you use run command to run any application?

20. Write short note on Control Panel.

21. How you can edit graphics in windows?

Read Author's new books

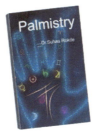
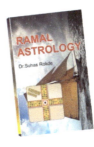
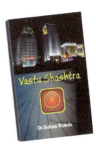

Dear Reader,

Thanks to read the book.

Your feedback is precious to us..

Write us at astrotechlab@gmail.com

Thanks & Regards

Author, Dr. Suhas Rokde

www.ingramcontent.com/pod-product-compliance
Lightning Source LLC
LaVergne TN
LVHW072049060326
832903LV00053B/298

* 9 7 8 1 7 2 0 0 2 7 5 2 2 *